A Journey Through Gender

A WORKBOOK FOR TEENS

© **Copyright 2022 - All rights reserved.**

The content contained within this book may not be reproduced, duplicated, or transmitted without direct written permission from the author or the publisher.

Under no circumstances will any blame or legal responsibility be held against the publisher, or author, for any damages, reparation, or monetary loss due to the information contained within this book, either directly or indirectly.

Legal Notice:

This book is copyright protected. It is only for personal use. You cannot amend, distribute, sell, use, quote or paraphrase any part, or the content within this book, without the consent of the author or publisher.

Disclaimer Notice:

Please note the information contained within this document is for educational and entertainment purposes only. All effort has been executed to present accurate, up to date, reliable, complete information. No warranties of any kind are declared or implied. Readers acknowledge that the author is not engaging in the rendering of legal, financial, medical, or professional advice. The content within this book has been derived from various sources. Please consult a licensed professional before attempting any techniques outlined in this book.

By reading this document, the reader agrees that under no circumstances is the author responsible for any losses, direct or indirect, that are incurred as a result of the use of information contained within this document, including, but not limited to, errors, omissions, or inaccuracies.

TABLE OF CONTENTS

Introduction 2
Identities 3
Emotion Wheel 5
Gender Beliefs 7
What is Gender? 10
Gender Questionnaire 13
Gender Expression 18
Pronouns 19
Outside Inside 21
From Gender Dysphoria to Gender Euphoria 26
Body Diary 27
Gender Euphoria 30
Outside Inside 31
Ways to Reach Euphoria 34
Loving Our Bodies 35
Affirmations 38
Reaching Out 44
Patience is Planning 51
Gender Questionnaire 57
Avenues of Affirmation 59
Next Steps 62
Envisioning Who We Want to Be 64
Resources 66
References 88

Introduction

"My identity is not a blind fortress, a breastplate behind which I hide to cut myself off from others. It is this window which belongs only to me, thanks to which I can discover the world."
– Alain de Benoist, 1943

Who are you? This is a crucial question that does not only pertain to what your name is. Think of all the things you identify as, a boy, girl, sister, brother, friend, student. There are endless titles to add to the list of what we are. And we are these things all at once. But why is it important to understand these labels? Why is it important to have an identity? What can we learn about the world through learning about our own identity?

In this workbook we will learn specifically about gender identity and its significance in understanding ourselves. For a long time, gender was known as 'male' and 'female'. But throughout the years we have unearthed many dimensions of gender and will continue to learn more about the different dimensions as time goes on. Just like our bodies, the understanding of gender is ever evolving. Learning about the uniqueness of everyone's gender experience will construct a space for compassion and openness so that we can explore and express who we really are.

"Identity is a process, identity is split. Identity is not a fixed point but an ambivalent point. Identity is also the relationship of the Other to oneself."
– Stuart Hall

Identities

Let us start by listing off all the things we identify as. You can be as creative as you like. Any label we want to give ourselves is an important part of our identity. This exercise is meant to show us how our identities contain multitudes!

If you are having trouble thinking of identities you feel comfortable using, feel free to utilize some of the ones listed on the next page.

WHAT DO YOU IDENTIFY AS?	WHY IS THIS IMPORTANT TO YOU?

IDENTITIES

Boy	Girl	Non-Binary	Trans	Sibling
Son	Daughter	Cousin	Friend	Your Nationality
Your Ethnicity	Generational Age Group	Student	Athlete	Artist
Musician	Gamer	Partner	Entrepreneur	Professional

As stated earlier, we can identify as any label we see fit. Some people like to use their ethnicity, gender, or nationality as part of their identity. Oftentimes, people will include their job title or hobby in their identity.

But it is important to remember that if you DO NOT want to identify yourself as those labels, that is okay too. Labels and identities are used so that others can better understand what we value in our lives. If you don't value what generational age group you were born into, you do not need to have that be in the forefront of your identifications.

Identities and labels can also be a tricky maze to navigate. Sometimes being labeled a certain thing can make others place you in societal boxes. Unfortunately it is the norm in this world to make assumptions about people based on what they label themselves as. It is a good practice to remember that labels and identities are not meant to be used as a means of discriminating, demeaning or shaming a person. We should strive to be in a world where everyone is proud about what it is they identify as. By choosing to see the beautiful and positive things associated with one's label, everyone can slowly learn to be comfortable with who they are.

Emotion Wheel

Learning about gender and exploring our own gender can sometimes be an emotionally taxing feat. While doing activities and learning about new topics, you may feel emotions that are both comforting but also some emotions that are uncomfortable. A lot of reflection and emotional charting will be required to understand more about our own gender identity. Throughout the workbook you will be asked to check in on how you are feeling and some of the causes of those feelings. Sometimes we don't always understand what feelings are running through us, but it is important to have the vocabulary to pinpoint what feelings we are experiencing.

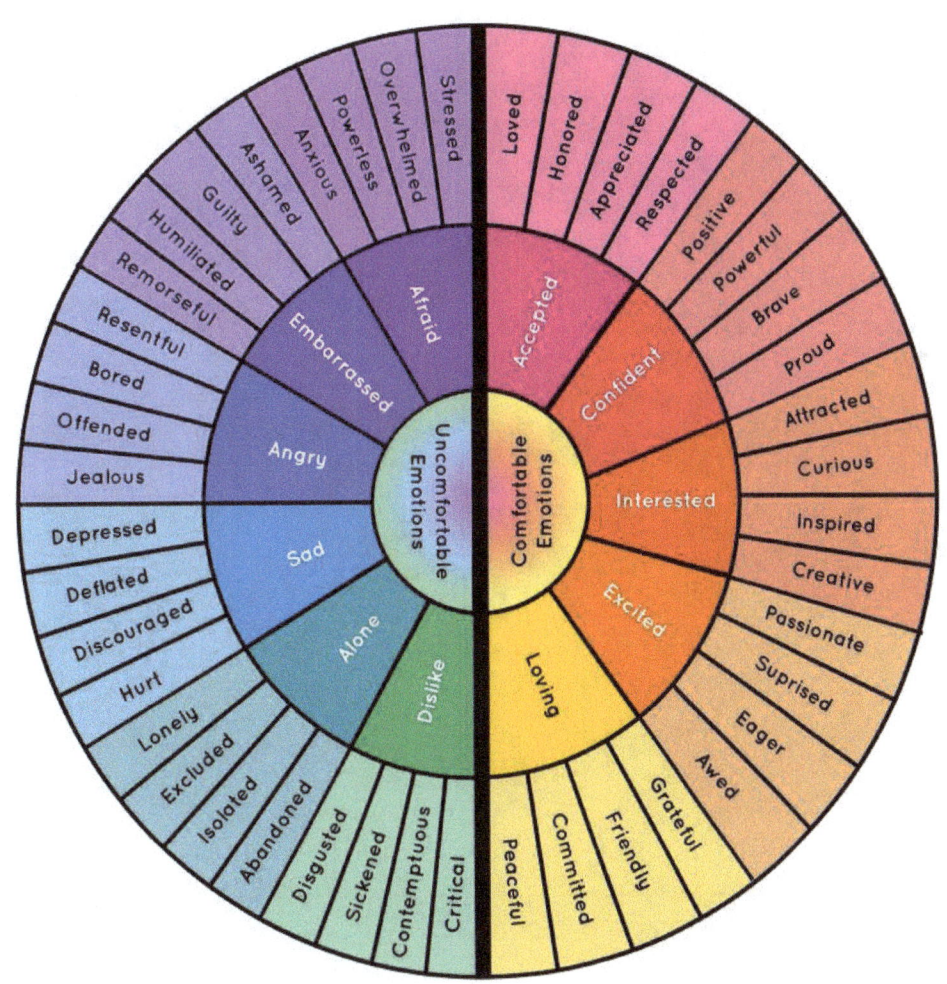

JOURNEY THROUGH GENDER

Below is a chart of emotions, and just like gender, the types of emotions are endless. But we can narrow down our feelings by first identifying if what we are feeling is a comforting emotion or an uncomfortable emotion. As you move towards the outside of the wheel, the emotions begin to get more specific.

As you progress through this workbook, you will be encouraged to note how you are feeling. Refer back to the 'Emotion Wheel' and go through the process of pinpointing where you are on the wheel. It is important that we note first whether the emotion is comfortable or uncomfortable, as well as the path that leads to the final emotion.

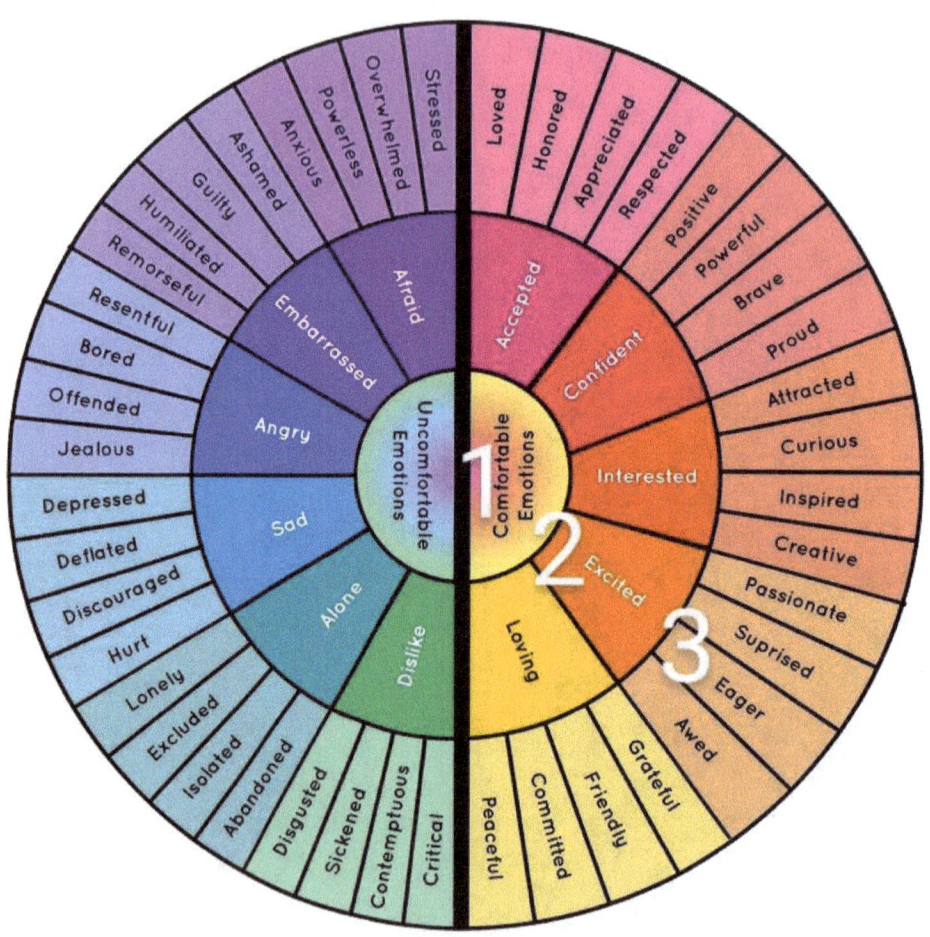

For example: Comfortable → Excited → Eager

LET'S TRY IT OUT!

How did you feel when you woke up this morning?
_____

How are you feeling right now?
_____

Gender Beliefs

We all have our own gender belief systems whether we notice them or not. At a young age there are a lot of things that society displays about gender that impact our own personal ideas. If you've never thought about your own gender beliefs, now is a great time to start. While it may seem backward to start with what we know about gender, before learning about gender, this is a way for us to track the way our ideas grow and change.

For this activity, write down today's date and start listing off your own gender beliefs. If you need help with finding out your beliefs, here are some questions to answer to help you find out!

DATE: _____

Write 3 physical traits that you believe are masculine.

_____
_____
_____

Write 3 physical traits that you believe are feminine.

_____
_____
_____

Write 3 emotional traits that are masculine.

_____
_____
_____

Write 3 emotional traits that are feminine.

_____
_____
_____

What are some jobs that only men can do?

_____
_____
_____

What are some jobs that only women can do?

_____
_____
_____

Why do you believe certain traits are more masculine?

_____
_____
_____

Why do you believe certain traits are more feminine?

_____
_____
_____

While everyone is entitled to their own gender beliefs, not everyone's beliefs are open to every person's gender journey. The purpose of this workbook is to help our beliefs about gender better encompass every person's experience. When we learn to expand what we believe about gender, we also learn to accept and love others more openly. The hope is to one day have a world where no one feels discomfort or stress over being who they want to be.

ROLES IN REVERSE

If you've written down what your gender beliefs are, try thinking about reversing those roles. Whatever you believe to be masculine, try imagining those traits on someone who is feminine. Chances are, we know someone who does not fall under the typical gender roles of male and female. Chances are, we know someone who lives their life outside the binaries of gender. Consider all the ways society has structured our beliefs about gender and reverse those roles.

REFLECTIONS

If you have specific ideas about masculinity and femininity, what in your life do you think influenced those ideas?

_____
_____
_____
_____

What is a trait you believe is neither masculine nor feminine?

_____
_____
_____
_____

How can traits be both?

_____
_____

CHECK IN

How did this exercise make you feel?

_____
_____
_____

What did you learn about yourself while doing this exercise?

_____
_____
_____

SUMMARY

It is easy to place people in certain categories for us to better understand them. But this oversimplifies the human experience. People usually don't find themselves in one box, but between the spectrum. Our identities are expansive and always changing and we cannot simply reduce a person to only one label when they have the ability to be many things, all at once.

It is beneficial to revisit our own gender beliefs once in a while and document the growth in our ideations. Again, this journey is expansive and ever evolving, just like you!

Gender is no longer a binary concept, but a full and beautiful spectrum. Our bodies are complex systems that can sometimes fit into certain categories, but other times do not. Recent studies have shown that at least 30 genes play a part in our sex development, and that the spectrum of gender goes beyond the connection between body and our reproductive functions. But before we can delve into our own gender, we must have a basic understanding of all the different types of gender.

A GENDER GLOSSARY

AGENDER	A person who does not identify with any gender.
ANDROGYNE	A person who identifies as both masculine and feminine.
CISGENDER	A person who identifies with the sex that they were assigned at birth.
GENDERFLUID	A person whose gender identity shifts between the gender spectrum. Some days they may identify more as a male and other days they may identify more as a female.
GENDERQUEER	A person who often identifies with a combination of genders or does not conform to binary identities.
NON-BINARY	A person who does not experience their gender outside the binary of male and female.
OMNIGENDER	A person who experiences all genders.
PAN/POLYGENDER	A person who identifies with multiple genders.
TRANSGENDER	A person who identifies as a gender outside the sex they were assigned at birth.
TWO SPIRIT	This is an umbrella term that encompasses different sexualities and genders in Indigenous Native American communities.

REFLECTION

Were you surprised by any of these terms? What gender have you not heard about before?
_____
_____

What gender do you identify with the most? You can identify with more than one of these terms.
_____
_____

Why do you believe that you are that gender? What about identifying with that gender makes you feel comfortable in it?
_____
_____

"Being transgender is not just a medical transition; it's discovering who you are, living your life authentically, loving yourself, and spreading that love towards other people and accepting one another no matter the difference."
— Jazz Jennings

Gender Questionnaire

PART 1

In this section of the workbook, you will be asked to answer a gender questionnaire to better gauge where you currently are in your gender journey. Nearing the end of this workbook, you will do this questionnaire again to see how you've grown or changed throughout this journey. Try to answer as honestly as possible. Think about how each question makes you feel and refer back to the Emotion Wheel when you are unsure.

DATE: _____

ASSIGNED GENDER: _____

GENDER IDENTITY: _____

Answer the questions below by placing an x in the box that best describes how you feel.

(Rarely, Never, Always, Often, Sometimes)

	R	N	A	O	S
In the last year, have you felt satisfied with your assigned gender?					
In the last year, have you felt uncertain about your gender identity?					
In the last year, have you felt pressured to act in a way you don't feel comfortable with, due to gender norms?					
In the last year, have you felt unsatisfied with your assigned gender?					

JOURNEY THROUGH GENDER

(Rarely, Never, Always, Often, Sometimes)   R   N   A   O   S

	R	N	A	O	S
In the last year, have you felt comfortable using public restrooms associated with your assigned gender?					
In the last year, have you had a desire to be a gender different than your assigned gender?					
In the last year have you been unhappy with your body?					
In the last year have you disliked your body because of the body parts that are associated with your assigned gender?					
In the last year, have you been happy with the way you present your gender identity?					

REFLECTION

How did answering these questions make you feel?

_____
_____

Did this gender questionnaire confirm any doubts you've had about your gender identity?

_____
_____

Do you think there are ways you can strengthen your gender identity? If so, how?

_____
_____

SUMMARY

Did you take note of how you felt during this activity? If there was any sort of discomfort, try to explore that area of discomfort. Journaling is a wonderful form of self-reflection and allows us to delve into what is happening in not only the exterior parts of our lives, but the interior parts as well. For the last section of this chapter, you will write a one page journal entry about your current experiences. Here are some questions you can answer while writing out this entry.

What have I learned so far?

_____
_____

Where am I in my gender journey?

_____
_____

How do I feel about my gender identity and how can that be enhanced?

_____
_____

What am I scared to tell loved ones about my gender identity? Why might I be scared to share that with loved ones?

_____
_____

How can I feel more supported through this process and who can help me feel that support?

_____
_____

JOURNEY THROUGH GENDER

GENDER JOURNAL ENTRY #1

DID YOU KNOW?

- 31% of non-binary people have experienced hate crime because of their gender identity.
- 25% of LGBT+ youth identify outside of two gender binaries.
- 12% of the overall millennial generation no longer see gender as male or female, fixed binaries.
- There will be 12–20% more non-binary people within the workplace within the next ten years.
- The APA (American Psychological Association) now claims that a person's "true self" is whatever that person believes him/herself to be regardless of the medical facts.
- One in three transgender people, and 48% of transgender men, have delayed or avoided preventive health care such as pelvic exams or STI screening out of fear of discrimination or disrespect.
- 9% of transgender people live in poverty, compared to 14% of the general population.
- Canada is the first country to collect and publish data on gender diversity from a national census.

As you can see, there is a sad truth that those living beyond the binaries of gender face a tougher life than the cisgendered, heteronormative population. This can be due to a number of factors. The lack of education regarding gender can cause fear and confusion to the general public. Learning about gender and the discrimination that the LGBTQIA2S+ community faces is one way we can learn to be true allies and support them in their fight for basic human rights.

Gender Expression

There are a lot of ways we are different from when we were born. From infanthood to adulthood we go through an array of changes in both our bodies and personalities. This may be true for our gender as well. When we are born, we are labeled with a gender within the binary of male and female. As we develop, we may not identify with that gender, or any gender at all. Some people live their whole lives feeling comfortable in the gender they were born in, but a lot of people don't. For some, our gender can feel like wearing old clothes. As time goes on, we outgrow our clothes and the clothes that once used to fit, now feel very uncomfortable. The clothes that we wear are still the same clothes, but we feel different in them. Some people may not present what gender they are feeling inside. Some people may seem comfortable with what they are presenting on the outside, but inside are experiencing severe discomfort.

This is part of understanding our own gender. What within, or outside the boundaries of gender, do we feel comfortable in? Ask yourself, does the way I feel inside look like how I present myself outside?

The way we choose to express our gender on the outside is called gender expression. Some people's gender expression may be different from their gender identity. Through clothes, makeup, hairstyles and accessories, we can present ourselves differently than how we feel on the inside.

Based on your gender identity, what are some ways you can express your gender?

_____
_____
_____
_____
_____

Pronouns

One of the many ways we can express our gender is through pronouns. Whether you know your pronouns or not, we use pronouns on an everyday basis. For many years, pronouns were always assumed, but not always correct. Although someone may look like a male, they might not identify as a "he/him." Understanding pronouns is a step in taking control of our own gender journey, and a way for us to respect other's journeys.

So what sort of pronouns are there?

SHE	HER	HER	HERS	HERSELF
HE	HIM	HIS	HIS	HIMSELF
THEY	THEM	THEIR	THEIRS	THEMSELVES
ZI	ZIR	ZIR	ZIRS	ZIRSELF
XE	XEM	XYR	XYRSELF	XEMSELF
ZE	HIR	HIR	HIRS	HIRSELF
PER	PER	PER	PERS	PERSELF

One of the biggest rules about pronouns is to NEVER assume what another person's pronouns are. Pronouns are sort of like a person's name, we don't usually assume what a person's name is. We always ask. Just like someone might not know your name when you first meet them. The way a person looks, or acts is never an indicator of the pronoun in which they identify.

REFLECTION

If you are unsure about your personal pronouns, here are some questions to ask yourself:

When you are referred to as "he/him" or "she/her," how does that make you feel?

_____
_____
_____
_____
_____
_____
_____
_____

What do you feel comfortable being called and why?

_____
_____
_____
_____
_____
_____
_____
_____

Write out an introduction statement that makes you feel most comfortable such as "Hello! My name is ____, my pronouns are ____."

_____
_____
_____
_____
_____
_____

Outside Inside

PART 1

For this next section, we are going to find creative ways to express how we are feeling on the outside, as well as the inside. In the first image, draw what you look like on the outside. Once that is finished, draw what you feel like on the inside. Feel free to use different mediums to express your creativity.

In the third image, draw what you want to feel like on the outside.

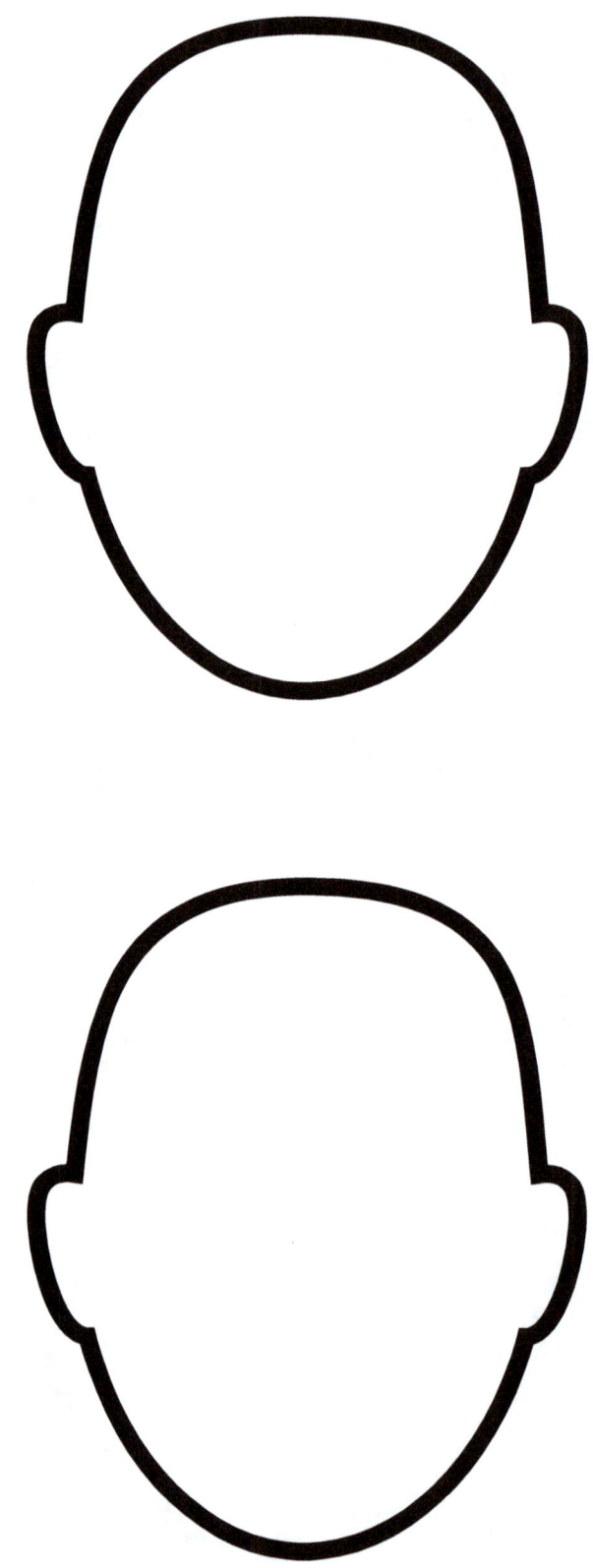

REFLECTION #3

How do the first and second drawings differ? How are they the same?

_____
_____
_____
_____

How do the first and third drawings differ? How are they the same?

_____
_____
_____
_____

If all three drawings could talk to one another, what would they say?

_____
_____
_____
_____

Is there harmony amongst the three images? Why or why not?

_____
_____
_____
_____

What are the ways you express your gender?

_____
_____
_____
_____

CHECK IN

_____
_____

What did you learn about yourself while doing this exercise?

_____
_____

SUMMARY

If you feel like there is dissonance between your body and mind, doing these exercises are a good way to learn the needs of your body and mental health. Try thinking of ways you can create harmony between your body and mind. Think about things that make you feel good on both the outside and inside. It does not just have to be clothes or makeup, but also activities. If dancing makes you feel good on both the outside and inside, that counts too! For the next journal entry, reflect on how the exercise made you feel, and why it made you feel that way. Consider the topics you learned about gender expression and pronouns and write about how that plays a part in your everyday life.

GENDER JOURNAL ENTRY #2

From Gender Dysphoria to Gender Euphoria

"The most common form of despair is not being who you are."
– Søren Kierkegaard

Gender dysphoria is a term used when a person's assigned gender (the gender they were assigned at birth), does not match their gender identity. Oftentimes people who experience gender dysphoria suffer from the feeling of discomfort in their body and feel a constant conflict with their self-image. The symptoms of gender dysmorphia can lead to depression, anxiety and low self-esteem. So it is very important that we are sensitive to other people's gender-journey.

We must also note that gender dysphoria is different from gender nonconformity. Which is a term used to describe a person who does conform to the binaries of gender.

It can be very difficult to be in a body we don't feel comfortable in. Similar to our previous analogy, it can be like wearing shoes that stopped fitting you years ago. If you or someone you know is dealing with gender dysphoria, there are many resources out there to cope with the feelings of discomfort. One of the first steps we can take when we recognize that we have gender dysphoria is talking to someone we unreservedly trust and recognizing that we are not alone in our gender journeys.

"Be who you are and say what you feel because those who mind don't matter and those who matter don't mind."
- Dr. Seuss

"I feel like my body is in a waiting room."
- Aimee Herman, Everything Grows

Tracking how our body feels physically and emotionally is a great way for us to gain self-awareness. Through self-awareness comes the confidence in reaching out for help when needed, and the ability to explain to others what it is we are going through.

For the next few days as you go through this workbook, fill out this body diary chart. You will note the date, and write three things your body is physically feeling, and three things you are emotionally feeling. In the last row, write out what might have caused what you are feeling. It can be as simple as 'bad day at school', or 'someone complimented me'.

This will help you gauge what triggers some of your emotions, good or bad. As the days go on you may notice more patterns about what you feel. Feel free to take note of that as well.

DATE:	PHYSICAL	EMOTIONAL	CAUSES
	1) 2) 3)	1) 2) 3)	
	1) 2) 3)	1) 2) 3)	

JOURNEY THROUGH GENDER

DATE:	PHYSICAL	EMOTIONAL	CAUSES
	1) 2) 3)	1) 2) 3)	
	1) 2) 3)	1) 2) 3)	

CHECK IN

What did you notice about how you were physically feeling throughout the week, and what you were emotionally feeling?

_____
_____

What patterns did you notice?

_____
_____

Were there certain triggers that made you feel a certain way this week?

_____
_____

DID YOU KNOW?

- 1924 - The Society for Human Rights is founded by Henry Gerber in Chicago. It is the first documented gay rights organization.

- July 1961 - Ilinois becomes the first state to decriminalize homosexuality by repealing their sodomy laws.

- December 15, 1973 - By a vote of 5,854 to 3,810, the American Psychiatric Association removes homosexuality from its list of mental disorders in the DSM-II Diagnostic and Statistical Manual of Mental Disorders.

- November 1995 - The Hate Crimes Sentencing Enhancement Act goes into effect as part of the Violent Crime Control and Law Enforcement Act of 1994. The law allows a judge to impose harsher sentences if there is evidence showing that a victim was selected because of the "actual or perceived race, color, religion, national origin, ethnicity, gender, disability, or sexual orientation of any person."

- 1974 - Elaine Noble is the first openly gay candidate elected to a state office when she is elected to the Massachusetts State legislature.

- 1974 - Kathy Kozachenko becomes the first openly LGBTQ American elected to any public office when she wins a seat on the Ann Arbor, Michigan City Council.

- October 11, 1988 - The first National Coming Out Day is observed.

- April 1, 1998 - Martin Luther King Jr.'s widow, Coretta Scott King, asks the civil rights community to help in the effort to extinguish homophobia.

Gender Euphoria

On one end of the gender spectrum, there is gender dysphoria, and on the other end there is 'gender euphoria'. A term used to describe a person's experience when they are able to feel bliss in their gender identity. It is beneficial for everyone to strive for 'gender euphoria' as a way for us to better accept, love and appreciate ourselves. Gender euphoria offers comfort in our bodies and is a sign of unity between our body and mind.

Reaching gender dysphoria can be a long and hard process. For some, it may take years. Learning to feel euphoric in our own bodies isn't something that everyone has the privilege to experience. But once someone does experience gender euphoria after years of suffering from gender dysphoria, it makes all our hard work seem worth it.

Outside Inside

PART 2

How can we shift ourselves to create that unity amongst our body and mind? To start, we can take the 'OUTSIDE INSIDE' activity that you did earlier and expand on it.

In the first image, draw what you look like on the outside. Once that is finished, draw what you feel like on the inside. Feel free to use different mediums to express your creativity. This time, add some of your favorite items, some of your favorite clothes and show the different ways you can express your gender identity. And finally, in the third image, draw what you want to feel like on the outside.

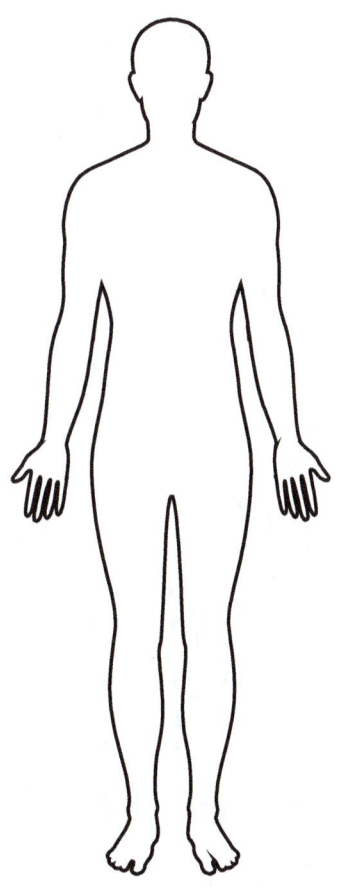

JOURNEY THROUGH GENDER

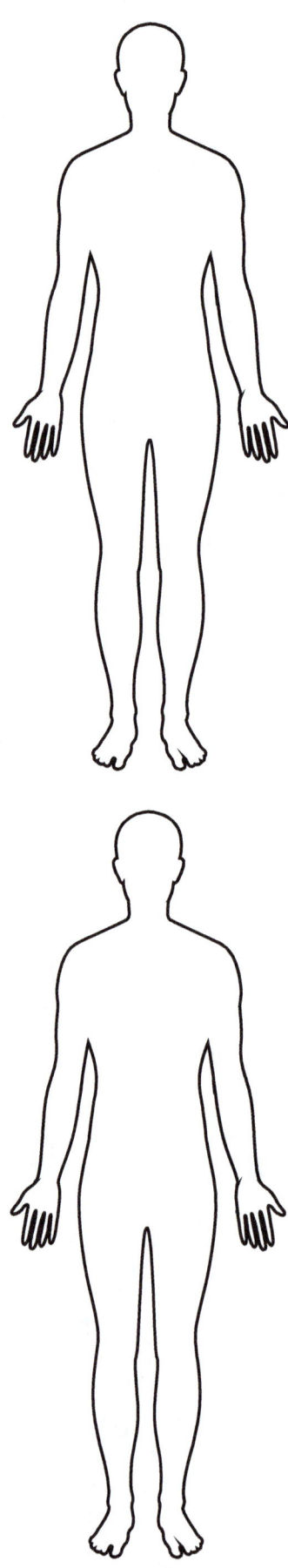

REFLECTION

How do the first and second drawings differ? How are they the same?

_____
_____
_____
_____

How do the first and third drawings differ? How are they the same?

_____
_____
_____
_____

If all three drawings could talk to one another, what would they say?

_____
_____
_____
_____

Is there harmony amongst the three images? Why or why not?

_____
_____

CHECK IN

How did this exercise make you feel?

_____
_____

What did you learn about yourself while doing this exercise?

_____
_____

Ways to Reach Euphoria

"How do I know who I am or where I am? How could a single wave locate itself in an ocean?"
– ***Rumi***

While going through this workbook, we must make sure we are caring for our mental health. With every exercise you do, it is important to check in with yourself and ask those hard questions. How am I feeling right now? What did I just learn about myself? If you don't have the answers to the check in's right at this moment, it is fine to revisit them once you've found some more insight.

At this point in the workbook, we should have established whether there is disconnect in our own bodies. There are people who go through their entire lives without any feeling of gender dysphoria, but there are a lot of people who do. And for those people with gender dysphoria, there are plenty of ways to strive for gender euphoria. If this is you, the first step is knowing that you are not alone.

But how can we start feeling unity in our bodies? How do we learn to cope with feelings of discomfort, depression or anxiety over our gender? In order to strive for euphoria, we must find avenues of compassion and self-love while practicing body positivity.

Loving Our Bodies

There are many variations in which a person can have a negative body image. While gender dysphoria can be the cause of body image issues, societal pressures, bullying or low self-esteem can lead to body image issues as well. Learning to love the body we were given, whether it is not in line with our gender identity, will help us cope through the discomfort of gender dysphoria.

This is not to say that we must accept our assigned gender even if we suffer from gender dysphoria. But the road between dysphoria to euphoria is not an easy one. This workbook is just a small step in making sure you are equipped with the right tools to make the ride a little more comfortable.

Every person is a unique and beautiful being. When we can learn to appreciate our own unique beauty, we will be able to treat our bodies with respect and compassion. Those two things are vital when going through a journey of self-discovery.

DID YOU KNOW?

- 36% of students from United Arab Emirates report being dissatisfied with their body.
- Body dysmorphic disorder symptoms are becoming increasingly common in male teenagers, with nearly 3% of the Australian population reporting body dysmorphic symptoms.
- Research has shown that around 50% of young 13 year old American girls reported being unhappy with their body. This number grew to nearly 80% by the time girls reached 17 years of age.
- Body image was listed in the top 4 concerns for young women.

AN ODE TO MY FRIEND

Sometimes it can be hard to be kind to ourselves. This is a problem that not only resides in figuring out our gender identity. A lack of self-compassion is a universal problem that many people deal with for a variety of reasons. Learning to praise yourself whenever possible is a really important step in learning to love and appreciate your body and mind and all it is able to do for you.

If you have a friend or family member who you love, you already know how to show kindness and compassion. For some it is easier to be kind and compassionate to those who we love, before learning to be kind to ourselves. So one way we can learn to shift the way we see ourselves is by starting to acknowledge ourselves as our own friend or loved one.

In this activity, you will write a letter to yourself as if you were talking to a friend. Address feelings you are going through and offer comfort and praise; just like you would when talking to a friend. Perhaps you can thank yourself for all the things you are capable of doing and write why you're grateful to have you as a friend.

DATE: _____

Dear: _____

_____
_____
_____
_____
_____
_____
_____
_____
_____
_____
_____
_____
_____

_____
_____
_____
_____

REFLECTION

In times of low self-esteem or depression, it can be difficult to see what there is to love in ourselves. But you are loved, whether it is by your parents, grandparents, or friends. Go to 3 people who you love and who love you. Ask them to give you 3 reasons you are special to them. It may help to tell them the 3 reasons they are special to you too!

PERSON	3 REASONS THEY LOVE ME

CHECK IN

How did talking to your loved ones about why they love you make you feel?

_____
_____
_____

Is this practice something you think would be beneficial to do again? If so, why?

_____
_____
_____

Affirmations

Another way we can practice self-love is through writing and reciting affirmations. Affirmations are a form of practicing positive thinking and self-empowerment. Some people use affirmations to meditate. Some people believe that self-esteem cannot be taught, but it can be bolstered and strengthened. Reminding ourselves of all the good we are a great form of strengthening our body image.

Here are some examples of positive thoughts and affirmations:

- I am strong
- I am smart
- Good things are going to come to me.
- I am enough
- I am in charge of my life
- I can make a difference
- Today I will forgive myself for my mistakes
- I deserve to be loved

Write seven positive affirmations. Each day, pick one of the affirmations you have written for yourself and focus on that affirmation.

MY AFFIRMATIONS

_____
_____
_____
_____
_____
_____
_____

A WEEK OF POSITIVE THINKING

For every affirmation you choose to focus on for the week, write a little journal entry expanding on that affirmation. Write this as early in the day as possible. This way you can keep it in mind as you are going through the day. Here are some questions to answer when writing out your entries.

- What are you going to try to do to make that positive affirmation?
- Why is this affirmation important?
- How are you going to display this affirmation during your day?

DAY 1

AFFIRMATION: _____

_____
_____
_____
_____
_____
_____
_____

DAY 2

AFFIRMATION: _____

_____
_____
_____
_____
_____
_____
_____

DAY 3

AFFIRMATION: _____
_____
_____
_____
_____
_____
_____

DAY 4

AFFIRMATION: _____
_____
_____
_____
_____
_____
_____
_____

DAY 5

AFFIRMATION: _____
_____
_____
_____
_____
_____
_____
_____

DAY 6

AFFIRMATION: _____
_____
_____
_____
_____
_____
_____

DAY 7

AFFIRMATION: _____
_____
_____
_____
_____
_____
_____

REFLECTION

How does thinking of yourself in a positive light make you feel?

_____
_____
_____
_____

At the end of the week revisit this activity. What have you learned about yourself through reciting your affirmations? What affirmations had the most effect on your mood throughout the week and why?

_____
_____
_____
_____

SUMMARY

So far you have explored many avenues of self-love and self-reflection. This does not mean that you magically attain a better body image. But it does mean that you now have some tools to work on your body image. The goal is to one day, look in the mirror, and feel unity with our body and minds. It is a lot of hard work to find yourself in place of peace with how you feel about your body. But practicing self-compassion will slowly chip away at the negative thoughts regarding your body image.

Try to revisit this part of the workbook when you are having a difficult day. On bad days, allow yourself the time to re-do these activities and track how they made you feel afterwards. Practice utilizing these activities in your daily life. Practice makes progress!

DID YOU KNOW?

- MRI evidence suggesting that certain neural pathways are increased when people practice self-affirmation tasks.
- Empirical studies show us that we can maintain our sense of self-integrity by affirming what we believe in positive ways.
- Affirmations have been shown to decrease health-deteriorating stress.
- Affirmations have been used effectively in interventions that led people to increase their physical behavior.
- Affirmations have been shown to help with the tendency to linger on negative experiences.
- Affirmations have been linked positively to academic achievement by mitigating GPA decline in students who feel left out at college.

GENDER JOURNAL ENTRY #3

Reaching Out

Reaching out to our support system can be a scary task. But it is a necessary one. A lot of people avoid talking to those closest to us about our inner pain. There is someone in this world that loves you for who you are, and who cannot wait to see the person you become. Whether that is your parents, siblings or friends. Finding the people who support us can increase our self-confidence. It can also allow us to go through difficult times with love and kindness. Just like you love and support someone in your life. There is bound to be someone in your life who can support you through your gender journey.

DID YOU KNOW?

- 80% of gay and lesbian youth in America report severe social isolation.
- In 2013, 92% of adults who are LGBT said they believe society had become more accepting of them than in the past 10 years.
- Young people who are LGBT and who are "out" to their immediate families report feeling happier than those who aren't.
- In July 2009, the Senate approved the Matthew Shepard Act, which outlaws hate crimes based on both sexual orientation and gender identity.
- 90% of teens who are LGBT come out to their close friends.
- While non-LGBT students struggle most with school classes, exams, and work, their LGBT peers say the biggest problem they face is unaccepting families.

MY FAMILY OF FIVE

Part 1

Think of five people who are very special to you. Five people who care for you and want what is best for you. This can be anyone from your family members to your friends, or even school faculty that you trust, like a teacher or school counselor. Remember, you deserve love and support!

Who are these five people?	What is their relationship to you?
_____	_____
_____	_____
_____	_____
_____	_____
_____	_____

It is okay if you cannot fill out the full five members. Think about the empty slots of people and as you go on in life, remember there is room for your current list to grow.

There are many ways in which people can support us. Whether they offer a listening ear, or advice, or comfort during tough times. Everyone in our lives plays important roles in our journey through self-development. Think about what each person in your support system can offer you, while bearing in mind what it is you need. While building our support system, it is good to think about why these people are important and what good they provide in your life.

MY FAMILY OF FIVE

Part 2

This next activity will ask you to write out some important things about our Family of Five. Remembering positive traits about them, as well as special moments with them is a good way to remind us why they are so important in our lives.

Fill out the chart below.

PERSON	3 FAVORITE THINGS ABOUT THEM	1 SPECIAL MEMORY WITH THEM	1 WAY THEY MAKE YOU FEEL LOVED
	1) 2) 3)		
	1) 2) 3)		
	1) 2) 3)		
	1) 2) 3)		
	1) 2) 3)		

WHAT DO YOU NEED?

What you need from each of the members in your support system can vary tremendously. Consider the way in which the person has made you feel loved, important, and heard. Build your needs from these people based on how they've helped you in the past. If a friend is really good at making you laugh, your need from them can be moments of relief or comfort during difficult times. If you have a sibling who is really good at listening, your need from them can be having them as a listening ear. Remember that each person on this list should be someone you care for, trust, and who trusts.

Fill out the chart below.

PERSON	WHAT YOU NEED FROM THEM

MY FAMILY OF FIVE

Part 3

In this next section, you will work on finding ways to reach out to these people about your gender journey. This may be the most difficult part of the workbook but reaching out to our loved ones is vital in finding avenues of love and support through this time in your life.

Consider everything you've written about your family of five. Write a short letter to each of these people incorporating what you've already written about them in previous activities. Structure your letter so that it mentions the 3 things you love most about them, one special memory you've had with them, and how they make you feel loved. Next, talk about your gender journey and what you are going through. Mention ways in which they can support you through this time.

PERSON 1: _____

DATE: _____

Dear _____

_____
_____
_____
_____
_____
_____
_____
_____
_____
_____
_____
_____
_____
_____
_____

PERSON 2: _____

DATE: _____

Dear _____

_____
_____
_____
_____
_____
_____
_____
_____
_____
_____

PERSON 3: _____

DATE: _____

Dear _____

_____
_____
_____
_____
_____
_____
_____
_____
_____
_____

PERSON 4: _____

DATE: _____

Dear _____

_____
_____
_____
_____
_____
_____
_____
_____
_____

PERSON 5: _____

DATE: _____

Dear _____

_____
_____
_____
_____
_____
_____
_____
_____
_____

SUMMARY

If you're nervous to reach out, don't worry about sending these letters to the designated person. This exercise was meant to give you the vocabulary to talk to people you care for about your gender journey. However, if you do feel that you want to send these letters out, that is a wonderful way to reach out for support.

While it might be hard to reach out about our own gender journeys, having a loving group of people to help you navigate through this journey will be one of the greatest things to come out of this. You may even find that your relationship with these people will grow even stronger.

Remember to be patient with yourself as well as with others. It may take time to get comfortable enough to reach out to our inner circle. And it takes time for your inner circle to understand what you are going through and how they can help.

Patience is Planning

While reaching out to someone sounds like an odd thing to plan for, if you are someone who has anxiety around talking to people, this may be a helpful outline for you. Below, we will work on planning your mission to reach out to at least one person in your support system.

First and foremost you have to know who you want to reach out to. Choose a person who has been there for you in the past. This person should be easy for you to talk to and should make you feel safe around them.

In this next section, you will write out a simple and tentative plan. The next few activities will help expand it into something that is full proof for you.

Fill out the chart below.

Who do you want to reach out to?	
When do you want to talk to this person?	
Where is the best place to have this conversation?	
Are the contents of this conversation confidential?	
What would you like this person to learn about you during this conversation?	
What is the best outcome that can occur from this conversation?	
What is the worst outcome that can occur from this conversation?	
What are your fears when talking to this person?	
How would you like to be supported by this person?	
How can they make you feel comfortable?	
What are some things you would like to hear from this person during this conversation?	
What are things you don't want to hear from this person during this conversation?	
Is there supplemental information or items you would like to give this person during this conversation? (ei, letters, support brochures, informative articles)	
What is the purpose of this conversation?	

If you had trouble answering any of the questions above, it is recommended to take a few days to think on those answers before moving forward.

SCRIPTING YOUR TALK

An easy way for you to be fully prepared for having a difficult conversation is to make an outline of what you are going to say. This way you can organize your thoughts and make it easy for the listener to understand. This can also give you the confidence you need in talking to your support system. When you know what you want to say and how you are going to say it, there is less likely chance that the conversation will be derailed by intrusive thoughts or tangents.

You may also find that it is helpful to know when you are going to say certain points and ideas. So, formulating your points in a particular order will be helpful in ensuring that you are as prepared as you can be to have this talk with your support system.

With all the questions you have answered so far in this section of the workbook, write a script of what you want to say to your peer about your gender journey. This can be in the form of a speech you will read to them or a letter that the person can read.

Use clear language and refer to any activity you have done so far in this workbook. Also feel free to refer back to the 'Emotion Wheel' to tell the person exactly what you are feeling about this gender journey.

_____
_____
_____
_____
_____
_____
_____
_____
_____
_____
_____
_____
_____

CHECK IN

How did working on this section make you feel?

What did you learn about yourself while doing this exercise?

TIPS FOR TALKING ABOUT YOUR GENDER IDENTITY

Don't rush. There are a lot of things to carefully consider when talking to someone about your gender identity. Knowing how to reach out and what to say in regard to your journey is not an easy thing to do. So take your time when preparing yourself for these talks. But also, take your time during these talks.

Be prepared for opposition. When talking to someone about yourself, you may come across someone who does not fully understand or agree with the journey you are on. Be ready to hear anything someone might say to you that may hurt your feelings. In the face of unkind words, remember to be firm in your identity and remember that you deserve love, kindness, and acceptance.

Be patient with others. Just like it might take a long time for you to come to terms with the gender identity you feel most comfortable in, it may also take time for your peers as well. Sometimes it just takes a little extra time for others to understand what you are going through, and that is okay.

Keep reaching out. While sometimes rejection happens, it is important that you continue to look for support wherever you can find it. Not everyone is surrounded by people who are accepting of us, but you can always search for new people who believe in you and support you.

SUMMARY

This section may be the most difficult to follow through with. Take your time in reaching out to people and remember that you deserve their help and support. It takes a village not only to raise a child, but to help that child become the best person they can be.

For the next journal entry, write about your experience reaching out to your peers. If you have not reached out yet, write about why that is. Are you fearful? Worried? Explore your emotions about talking to your support system.

JOURNEY THROUGH GENDER

GENDER JOURNAL ENTRY #4

Gender Questionnaire

PART 2

This workbook asks for a lot of personal growth. Now that you have learned about the gender spectrum, gender expression and ways to reach out about your gender journey, you have already made great progress in better understanding yourself.

It is expected, but not required, that your views on your own gender have changed at this point. So in this section of the workbook, we will revisit the gender questionnaire you filled out in the beginning. Try to answer as honestly as possible. Think about how each question makes you feel and refer back to the Emotion Wheel when you are unsure.

This time the questionnaire will focus on your gender journey since the start of this workbook.

DATE: _____

ASSIGNED GENDER: _____

GENDER IDENTITY: _____

Answer the questions below by placing an x by the box that best describes how you feel.

(Rarely, Never, Always, Often, Sometimes)

	R	N	A	O	S
Since you started this workbook, have you felt satisfied with your assigned gender?					
Since you have started this workbook, have you felt uncertain about your gender identity?					
Since you started this workbook, have you felt pressured to act in a way you don't feel comfortable in, due to gender norms?					

(Rarely, Never, Always, Often, Sometimes)   R   N   A   O   S

Question	R	N	A	O	S
Since you have started this workbook, have you felt unsatisfied with your assigned gender?					
Since you have started this workbook, have you felt comfortable using public restrooms associated with your assigned gender?					
Since you have started this workbook, have you had a desire to be a gender different than your assigned gender?					
Since you have started this workbook, have you been unhappy with your body?					
Since you have started this workbook, have you disliked your body because of the body parts that are associated with your assigned gender?					
Since you have started this workbook, have you been happy with the way you present your gender identity?					

REFLECTION

How did doing this questionnaire a second time make you feel?

_____
_____
_____

Did your answer differ from the first time? If so, why do you think that is? If not, why do you think that is?

_____
_____
_____

What are things you have learned about yourself while doing this questionnaire?

_____
_____
_____

Avenues of Affirmation

Affirmation is not just positive phrases we tell ourselves. Affirmation can go far beyond our words. It is about accepting someone for who they are and learning to love a person beyond their exterior. To be affirmed in your gender identity is to be fully seen for what you want to be seen as, and to be received with kindness and compassion.

DISMISSIVENESS – TOLERANCE – AFFIRMATION

On one end of the spectrum there is dismissiveness. This is to be completely overlooked. When someone does not recognize your identity or chooses not to see who you are, they are being dismissive. Dismissing others and dismissing ourselves is a dangerous trait to practice. It ignores the humanity of a person and denies them of their ability to express who they want to be.

Tolerance is another form of dismissal; however, it is a trickier outlook to pinpoint on a person. Tolerance is when someone acknowledges your identity, but rather than affirming it, they choose to just allow you to be who you are without recognizing you as important, valuable, special or lovable. Tolerance comes in many obscure forms. Most of the time it can manifest out of someone's passive aggressive behaviors toward you or can show itself when someone constantly forgets your correct pronouns, name or gender identity.

Affirmation is the end goal. Affirming someone's identity is the complete opposite of dismissiveness and tolerance. Affirming others means loving them for who they want to be and accepting them as they are. Being affirmed by others can feel euphoric and can make your gender journey a better and more meaningful experience.

REFLECTION

Describe a time when someone was dismissive towards you. How did it make you feel?

_____
_____
_____
_____

Describe a time when someone tolerated you. How did it make you feel?

_____
_____
_____
_____

Describe a time when someone affirmed your identity? How did it make you feel?

_____
_____
_____
_____

REFLECTION

Describe a time when you were dismissive to another person. How do you think that made them feel? How could you have been more affirming towards them?

_____
_____
_____
_____

Describe a time when you truly affirmed a person? How did that make you feel? How do you think that made them feel?

_____
_____
_____
_____

WHY IS AFFIRMATION IMPORTANT?

Affirmation plays a huge role in our gender identities. When someone is scared to let others know about their journey, they are taking in their gender identity, it is likely that they are fearful of not being fully affirmed by their peers. If everyone was accepted and loved no matter what their gender identity was, exploring our gender or sexuality would not be such a difficult process to go through. When we affirm others, accepting them for what they want to be, it then makes it easier for us to affirm ourselves.

Affirmation can overcome and eradicate discrimination of any sort. It can also build strong communities of diverse groups of people. This is the world we should strive to live in. When you affirm someone, you are telling them "I see you. I value you. You are an important and beautiful part of this world." And doesn't that sound like what we would like to hear from others as well?

For the next journal entry, write about your experience with affirmation. Why do you think affirmation is important and how it has affected your life. Discuss ways you can affirm others in your everyday life.

GENDER JOURNAL ENTRY #5

_____
_____
_____
_____
_____
_____
_____
_____
_____
_____
_____
_____
_____
_____
_____

_____

_____

_____

_____

_____

_____

_____

_____

_____

_____

_____

_____

Next Steps

SO WHERE DO YOU GO FROM HERE?

In the last few chapters, we have delved into ways we can build communities while learning to communicate your needs to those in your inner circle. Exploring your gender identity is not easy, but it is not something you need to go through alone. There are many resources for you to better understand yourself, as well as resources to help you through difficult times. While those in our inner circle are there to help us, sometimes it is beneficial to reach out beyond our inner circle for support.

Here are some ways we can reach out for support outside of our immediate support system.

1. Talk to a counselor. Our schools are equipped with professionals who can offer help during hard times. Talking to your school counselor may be a great way to find other forms of help and resources.

2. Consider therapy. Talk to your parents about getting a therapist. If you deal with anxiety and depression, therapy can help you grow the tools you need to cope with difficult feelings. It can strengthen your self-esteem, as well as help you identify the source of some of your mental health issues. This is also something you may want to consider as a family. Family therapists can facilitate healthy conversations between you and your parents so that they better understand how to help you through your gender journey.

3. Look for support groups. Some schools offer after school groups that bridge the gap between the heteronormative and the LGBTQIA2S community. Clubs like the Gay Straight Alliance (GSA) is a common school club that can connect you with other students who are going through similar situations as you.

4. Look for similar stories. Whether in person or online, there are thousands of teenagers who are experiencing a similar gender journey as you. Reading up on other people's experiences allow us to feel like we are not alone in our problems. Taking the time to listen to someone who is also experiencing difficulties in discovering their gender identity can offer you a community that can grow together and learn together.

Envisioning Who We Want to Be

Consider all that you have learned while going through this workbook. At this point you should have some ideas of the person you want to become and what you want out of this gender journey. Perhaps you have come to terms with the ways you want to achieve your gender identity. Or maybe you have confirmed your feelings of wanting to transition into the opposite gender. All of these are brave processes to tackle.

In this next section, you will work on building the image of who you want to become, as well as acknowledging who you are.

Using the same outline from the previous OUTSIDE INSIDE activity, draw what you want to become. Whether that is a gender-fluid person, or a trans-person.

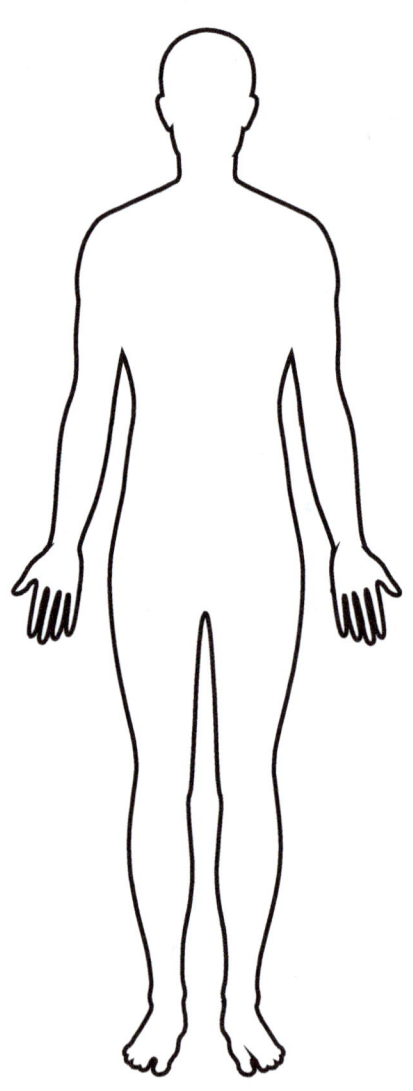

JOURNEY THROUGH GENDER

In this next outline, write out all the identities you hold within you inside this outline. Refer to the beginning of the book to find terms that suit your identity.

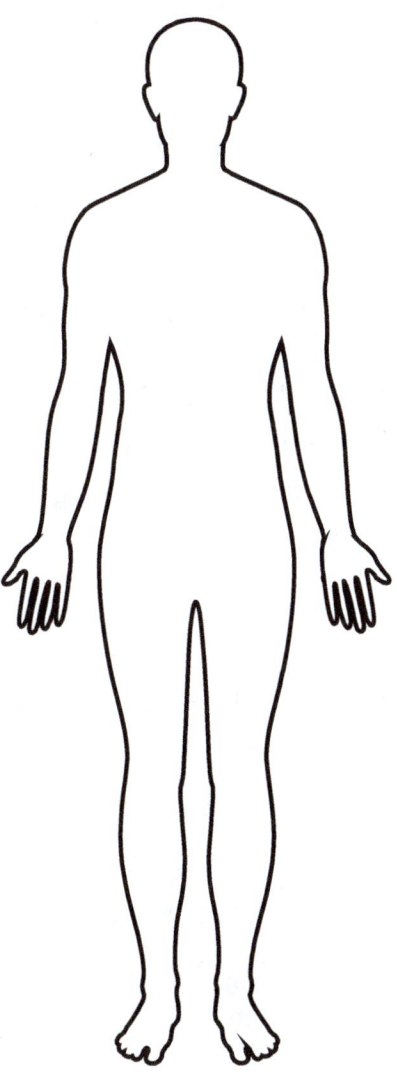

CHECK IN

How did this exercise make you feel?

_____
_____

What goal do you have for your gender identity?

_____
_____

Resources

There are many resources outside of this workbook to aid in your gender journey. Some resources are specific to youth who want to transition their gender, or youth who want to encompass a more gender-fluid identity. Having these resources on hand is a great way to equip ourselves and those around us with the tools to grow in our understanding of gender.

As the years go on, more people are coming out to the public about their sexuality and gender identity. Seeing positive representation in the media gives people in the LGBTQIA2S+ community hope for a better future. It also pushes back against the degrading culture we live in and sheds light on the beauty of that community.

BOOKS

Reading books with similar stories to your own is a wonderful way to find connections outside of social circles. When we see our stories in other people's lives, it helps validate our struggles and gives us a sense of hope. If you plan on transitioning, reading memoirs from people who have transitioned will help you find support and different avenues of success. It will also make the journey seem less lonely. Not that long ago, books with gender-queer characters, or books that shed light on the LGBT community were hard to find. Now there are thousands of books on the market by strong people sharing their gender journey with the public. Use their stories to build yours.

If you don't know any books about gender identity, here are a few to start:

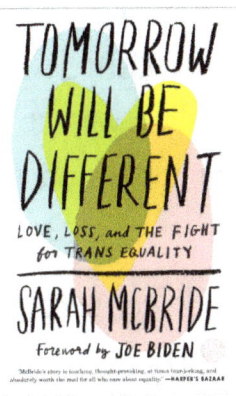 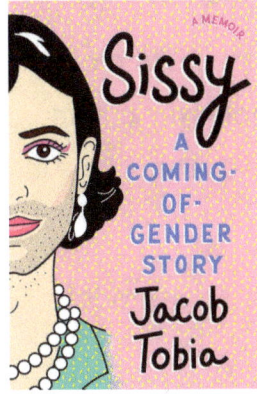  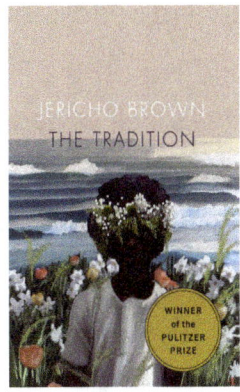

"Tomorrow Will Be Different" by Sarah McBride / "Sissy" by Jacob Tobia / "Felix Ever After" by Kacen Callender / "The Tradition" by Jericho Brown / "Trans Like Me" by CN Lester / "It Feels Good to be Yourself" by Theresa Thorn / "Trans Love" an anthology / "Beyond the Gender Binary" by Alok Vaid-Menon

 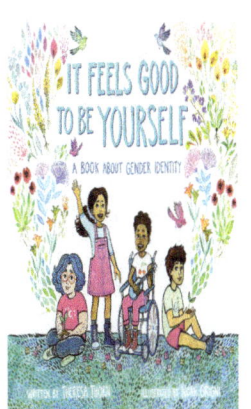 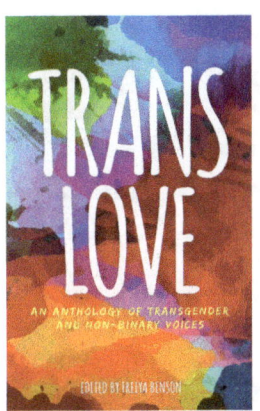 

DOCUMENTARIES

Watching documentaries about the LGBTQIA2S+ experience is the one of the most riveting ways to delve deep into the struggles of gays, lesbians, trans or non-binaries. The great thing about movies is that we can watch them with our peers. So plan a movie night and watch this heartbreaking, but inspiring documentaries. If you feel uncertain about what someone in your inner circle may feel about your gender journey, showing them a documentary with facts and true stories might help you gauge where they are in truly accepting who you want to become.

"The Case Against 8" / "The Death and Life of Marsha P. Johnson" / "Disclosure" / "Freeheld" / "Portrait of Jason" / "We Were Here" / "How to Survive a Plague" / "Word is Out"

PODCASTS

Listening to podcasts about a community you belong to can expand your knowledge and self-development. There are hundreds of podcasts out there dedicated to sharing LGBTQIA2S+ stories. As well as podcasts that discuss the struggles the community faces and ways to cope with those struggles. So while on a walk, or just before bed, tune into some podcasts and expand your worldview about your community.

Here are some podcasts you can find on Spotify or Apple Podcasts if you just don't know where to start!

MEDIA IN ME

A Month of MY Media

Over the next month, you will consume media created or about the LGBTQIA2S+ community. Once a week, listen to a podcast, watch a documentary, or listen to music made by this community. If you don't know what to consume, there are plenty of amazing recommendations to start with in the previous pages.

Choose one piece of media to consume a week. And at the end of the week, fill out the chart below:

WEEK 1

What media did you consume?	What did you learn?	How did this piece of media make you feel?	Who do you want to share this media with and why?

WEEK 2

What media did you consume?	What did you learn?	How did this piece of media make you feel?	Who do you want to share this media with and why?

WEEK 3

What media did you consume?	What did you learn?	How did this piece of media make you feel?	Who do you want to share this media with and why?

WEEK 4

What media did you consume?	What did you learn?	How did this piece of media make you feel?	Who do you want to share this media with and why?

REFLECTION

What sort of media did you enjoy the most?

_____
_____

What did you learn about yourself while you consumed this media?

_____
_____

GENDER JOURNAL ENTRY #6

_____
_____
_____
_____
_____
_____
_____
_____
_____
_____
_____
_____
_____
_____
_____
_____
_____
_____

_____
_____
_____
_____
_____
_____
_____
_____
_____

SUMMARY

Congratulations! You have done tremendous work in exploring your gender journey. But it isn't over yet. As you get older, your gender journey will evolve and the world around you will change. This workbook is the tiniest of steps toward feeling better in our body and accepting what our true gender identity is.

By this point you have already learned most of the basic terms regarding gender identity and learned tools to track your emotions and cope with the struggles of gender dysmorphia. If you continue to struggle, know that you don't need to go through this journey alone. Talk to a trusted peer or adult. Or if you've come this far, and still are feeling doubt towards what you want to do in your gender journey, feel free to show your loved ones some of the activities you've completed. Perhaps this can help you talk to your loved ones about your struggles with gender, or perhaps it can show them how far you've come! Know that this journey you are on is a brave one to take. And you deserve to explore it with support, love and compassion.

Because the journey isn't over yet, there are a few pages at the end of this workbook to journal in. You can use it however you like, whether that is for notes, or answering some journal prompts. On the next page will be some helpful journal prompts you can use.

JOURNAL PROMPTS

- When did you first become aware of the changes in your gender identity? What was that like? Can you recall memories of this time?
- If you could envision a world that fully accepts, loves and respects you, what would that look like?
- What does the LGBTQIA2S+ community mean to you?
- Who is some gender-queer celebrities you look up to and why? How have they encouraged you?
- What are your favorite things about your body?
- What makes you happy?
- Write a letter to your younger self.
- Write a letter to your future self.
- What would you say to someone who is anti-LGBTQIA? How would you respond to them with grace?
- What has been the biggest obstacle in your gender journey? Have you overcome it? If so, how? If not, what are ways you can do to make that obstacle smaller?
- What are you most proud of?
- Describe a time you felt discriminated against because of your gender identity? What did you do at that moment? What could you have done differently?
- What are ways you can spread pride for your gender identity?
- What are some of your emotional triggers?
- Who is someone in your personal life that you look up to and why?
- How can you find creative ways to express your gender?
- What does gender euphoria look like to you? How do you know when you've achieved that?
- What does your gender look like to you? How would you change your body to better encompass your gender identity?

NOTES/JOURNAL ENTRIES

References

DID YOU KNOW?

16 FACTS about Gender Dysphoria/Gender Identity Disorder. (n.d.). Real Impact Help Center. https://intercom.help/real-impact/en/articles/3499539-16-facts-about-gender-dysphoria-gender-identity-disorder

The Daily — Canada is the first country to provide census data on transgender and non-binary people. (n.d.). https://www150.statcan.gc.ca/n1/daily-quotidien/220427/dq220427b-eng.htm

Zabriskie, M. (2022, October 23). LGBTQ Rights Milestones Fast Facts. CNN. https://edition.cnn.com/2015/06/19/us/lgbt-rights-milestones-fast-facts/index.html

Linardon, J. (2022, February 27). Body Image Statistics 2022: 47+ Shocking Facts & Stats. Break Binge Eating. https://breakbingeeating.com/body-image-statistics/

EMOTION WHEEL

Human Systems. (2022, December 2). Emotion Wheels & Needs Wheel. https://humansystems.co/emotionwheels/

OTHER

Thomas. (2011). Play and Art Therapy Interventions for Gender Nonconforming Children and Their Families.

Harmful Stereotypes Worksheet. (n.d.). https://enseignerlegalite.com/wp-content/uploads/2019/09/Harmful-Stereotypes-Worksheet-Handout.pdf.

Seattle and King County. (2016). Sexual Orientation and Gender Identity. https://www.wlwv.k12.or.us/cms/lib/OR01001812/Centricity/Domain/2721/Sexual%20Orientation%20and%20Gender%20Identity.pdf.

Corrington, D. R. (n.d.). Outside/Inside Masks. https://arttherapydirectives.blogspot.com/2012/08/outsideinside-masks.html?fbclid=IwAR1T6ftiI3QRJzHsE5L9d-v95UTgWWmP7MJK6JHFK5X_yWfmCEPB6bECt8U

Sex and Gender Identity | A guide through the history of sexuality and gender identity. (n.d.). https://blogs.baylor.edu/genderidentity/

Wheel, G. (2022, November 9). Coloring Pages & Posters. The Gender Wheel. https://www.genderwheel.com/coloring-pages-and-posters/

Must-Read Books by Transgender, Non-Binary, and Gender Non-Conforming Authors | Penguin Random House. (n.d.). PenguinRandomhouse.com. https://www.penguinrandomhouse.com/the-read-down/books-by-trans-non-binary-and-gender-non-conforming-authors/

GIDYQ-AA (Female Adolescent Version).pdf. (n.d.). Google Docs. https://drive.google.com/file/d/0B0v37uLM6ugbMkp0WnVTVUVJLUE/view?resourcekey=0-_H1sSumypZufjVD8DL5Rhw

www.ingramcontent.com/pod-product-compliance
Lightning Source LLC
LaVergne TN
LVHW081543060526
838200LV00048B/2196